D0576472

McCall Collection of Modern Art

Modern American—
Op, Pop, and the School of Color

by SAM HUNTER

Published by Fratelli Fabbri Editori,
Publishers, Milan, Italy, and

The McCall Publishing Company
New York, New York

Illustrations Copyright ©1970, in Italy,
by Fratelli Fabbri Editori, Milan, Italy

PUBLISHED IN ITALY UNDER THE TITLE
Mensile d'Arte
ALL RIGHTS RESERVED. PRINTED IN ITALY
Library of Congress Catalog Card Number: 78–106651
SBN 8415–1005–9

Abstract Expressionism

The first painting movement that brought American artists worldwide attention and recognition was Abstract Expressionism, or in Harold Rosenberg's evocative epithet coined in 1951, "Action Painting." These descriptive terms cover a loose association of artists guided by common aims who emerged just after World War II in a period when the School of Paris seemed to be vacant of new ideas and dying of skill. The decline in the pace of European innovation during the forties, with the possible exception of Dubuffet and Giacometti, and catastrophic public events on the Continent had the paradoxical effect of releasing new energies among young American artists. For a moment, it even seemed that the impulse of modernism had been expatriated and driven underground in this country, for the emerging American vanguard drew support and inspiration in its complex beginnings from the presence in New York during the war years of a number of Europe's leading artists and intellectuals. Léger, Tanguy, Mondrian, André Breton, Ernst, and Matta, to mention a few, maintained warm and influential relationships with many of the younger Americans, and bridged the intimidating distance between themselves and European modernism. A number of these European artists showed at the Art of this Century Gallery of Miss Peggy Guggenheim, and it was there that the pioneer American Abstract Expressionists, Pollock, Rothko, Still, Hofmann, Motherwell, and Baziotes, held their first one-man shows between the years 1943 and 1946.

Jackson Pollock's exhibition of 1943 was the first in the series of the new vanguard representations, and, in retrospect, it takes on the character of a visual manifesto for a new point of view in American art. Pollock was for some time mistakenly identified with the artistic productions shown in the same gallery of the European Surrealists, and his rather narrow and violent early painting did in fact show obvious relationships to Surrealist automatism and symbolism. At the same time, Robert Motherwell was also testing "automatic" painting, and Arshile Gorky worked directly under the influence of Matta and Miró's abstract Surrealism. Baziotes, Rothko, Gottlieb, Still, and Newman explored archaic and primitivist art forms and turned to "myth" for a new subject matter. Their originality lay in an emphasis on symbolic content not for its historical or nostalgic association, but as a way of relating the findings of the unconscious mind to the act of creation itself. It was some time, however, before fantasy and personal expressiveness were purged and transcended in their art.

In his early style Pollock wrestled with crude and vital fantasies derived mainly from the imagery of Picasso's *Guernica* and Surrealism, but a free and powerful brush dissolved his content of violence, subtly transforming it into the nonrepresentational "writing" that later became his recognizable trademark. Even his open, drip paintings after 1947, however, still echoed the charging energies and conflicting moods of these first imagistic paintings. In the labyrinthian coils of his whipped lines, some imaginary beast or an invisible adversary seemed trapped and struggling to free itself. Surrealism to a lesser degree formed the paintings of Willem de Kooning, who shared with Pollock leadership of the American avant-garde and after 1952 became its most influential figure. His first imagery was essentially fantastic in content, too, but it is only a short step in de Kooning's art from such images rooted in the Surrealist imagination to the fragmented and freely registered color-shapes of his mature style. After 1948, the fantasies are still there but subdued and incorporated within a larger presence.

The process of sublimating fantasy and violent, expressionistic accents also brought visible change in the work of other members of the American vanguard in the late forties. Rothko, Newman, Gottlieb, and Still abandoned myth and primitivistic content for purely abstract idioms. Painting discovered new resources in elucidating the creative act itself as its primary expressive content. There was a shift in emphasis, then, from what was taking place inside the artist's mind to the developing image that grew under his hand. In the process, the artist inevitably became something of a virtuoso performer, inviting his audience to admire his skill in improvisation, his boldness in gambling all his chips, as it were, on a moment of great intensity and brief duration.

This was true particularly of Pollock, Hofmann, and de Kooning, and other artists associated with them who gave special importance to speed of execution and autographic gesture. Their work embodied a new time sense, for it insisted that the painting be experienced urgently as an action and an immediate concrete event. The painting thus came to symbolize an incident in the artist's drama of self-definition rather than an object to be perfected, a fantasy to be expressed, or a structure to be made in accordance with certain preset rules. The term *action painting* has moral implications of engagement, and esthetic meaning as a liberation from received ideas of "style" that carry beyond the question of athleticism and improvisatory energy to which this epithet has generally been restricted.

The German modernist Hans Hofmann, whose influence as a teacher on the American vanguard was immense, was perhaps the first artist to anticipate the freer modes of action painting. As early as 1940, in the innovating painting *Spring,* he explored the technique of dripping and flinging paint on the canvas surface, a method that Pollock later canonized. Hofmann later distinguished in conversation between traditional concepts of fixed form, and the idea of mobile form that serves a process of continuous transformation and spatial movement. In his own work, paint stroke, mark, and drip instantly registered as coherent and intelligible form when they hit the canvas surface. This, of course, was the generic type of painting that revolutionized American art in the forties. First a widening circle of artists, then a small group of critics and connoisseurs, and finally a wider public acquired the capacity of "reading" action painting and its related sculpture in welded metals as a new and complete esthetic statement.

The transition in style from various forms of expressionist and romantic Realism, which dominated the period of the thirties, to the new abstraction was for most of the vanguard artists rather abrupt. Apart from Gorky, Hofmann, and de Kooning, most of the new generation were mature artists who had worked effectively as interpreters of the social scene before their conversion to abstract idioms. It is significant that in the forties and early fifties representational imagery reappeared in their work with frequency and intensity. Pollock's early anatomical fantasies were restored in his black-and-white paintings of 1951, as if he were compelled to repeat his rite of passage from figuration to abstraction, in order to prevent any confusion with purist or intellectualized forms of nonobjective art established earlier in the century. A romantic and expressionist bias was erupting within an abstract manner at the same period in Europe in the primitivistic figuration of Dubuffet and in the grotesque inventions of Jorn, Appel, and the Cobra group. Only the human mask, the human body, or a fantastic bestiary seemed able to deal with the intensity of feeling that this painting "of extreme situations" on both sides of the Atlantic took for its prinicpal content.

From the late forties until the middle fifties, de Kooning acted as the dominant force in American painting, providing a dictionary of vital pictorial ideas and a point of departure for new explorations. Pollock's liberating energies and formal radicalism gave him a status of culture hero for young artists, and his untimely death in 1956 expanded the legend. But his direct influence was negligible until the deeper meanings of his style became apparent at a later date. It was de Kooning's painterliness, his combination of aggressive onslaught on the grand manner and traditional reminiscence, his elegance in a pictorial environment of violence that far more directly affected his own and a transitional generation of younger artists. The open de Kooning "image," with its repudiation of "style" and studio professionalism, left room for the refined lyricism of Jack Tworkov, the structured fluencies in paint and collage of Esteban Vincente, and distinct personalizations of his idiom among an emerging crop of brilliant young painters, Larry Rivers, Joan Mitchell, Grace Hartigan, Al Leslie, and others. Their manners were too abrasively individual to be homogenized in a school, in the academic sense, yet sufficiently representative to give de Kooning's brand of Abstract Expressionism the solidarity and authority of a genuine movement. As Harold Rosenberg has stated, with his usual perceptiveness, in the book *The Anxious Object*, vital art movements release rather than stereotype individual energies. "In the shared current, individuality, no longer sought for itself, is heightened.... Far from constricting the artist's imagination, the movement magnetizes under the motions of his hand insights and feelings from outside the self and perhaps beyond the consciousness."

As Abstract Expressionism gained currency in regional centers, it seemed identified almost exclusively with the physiognomy of the de Kooning painting, whether abstract or figurative, and for a long while the important innovations of another associated but widely divergent group of pioneer American Abstractionists were diminished and denied their full importance. The painters Clyfford Still, Mark Rothko, Barnett Newman, later to be joined by Adolph Gottlieb after his "pictograph" phase, brought to American art a Symbolist abstraction that has become as formative an influence in the sixties as the de Kooning manner was in the fifties. Although they openly rejected the methods and aims of action painting, there were strong ties between the two groups of artists, quite apart from intimate personal association.

In the constellation of painters identified with de Kooning and Pollock, action painting presented itself as an art of passionate gesture, mobility, and large liberties. The painting could be understood as the record of the creative act, for the vital signs of personal involvement and spontaneous invention were left conspicuously visible to document the artist's process of esthetic decsion-making. However, by the late forties, the charged expressive brushwork of the orthodox action painters and their vehement emotional accents had significantly given way to breadth, refinement, and objectivity.

Pollock's open, drip paintings absorbed incident, image, and eruptive details to a field of uniform accents. As recognizable image fragments and points of psychological stress and violence in paint handling were submerged, the overall effect of the painting gained in importance. The entire, evenly accented painting rectangle achieved a single, "overall" effect, or totality, and arranged itself in the eye of the beholder as one palpitant, shimmering whole. With this development came an increase in scale, and thereby in impressiveness, with the result that in addition to operating as an absorbing spectacle of gesture, the painting seemed to expand out beyond the limits of the frame, putting the spectator in an "environmental" situation. Pollock's great paintings of 1949 and 1950, and de Kooning's monumental works such as *Excavation* and *Attic* of the same period, are not to be considered mere gestural display or an athletic, virtuoso performance. They are too large, profound, and deeply meditated structures for a restricted reading as expressionist outbursts. They are, in fact, attempts to confront a total environmental situation, as were Monet's late waterscapes, in a more passive and optical manner. Sheer physical extension erases the boundaries between the work of art and the space we, the audience, occupy.

But the intuition of an expansive, uniform pictorial field and a more monolithic kind of order was already at work in the even more radical styles of Clyfford Still, Mark Rothko, and Barnett Newman, whose art, by the late forties, was positioned at the antipodes of energetic action painting, with its particular emphasis on drawing, dissociation of form, and personal gesture. Where Pollock and de Kooning achieved spatial envelopment by the acceleration and fragmentation of form and image, these artists gained a potent expansive force by deceleration of small, variegated forms into dominant islands, zones, and boundless fields of intense, homogeneous color. In place of motor activity of the hand, illusionistic and optical ambiguities were utilized to express qualities of changefulness.

Some of these significant changes can be experienced in Barnett Newman's immense red color-field in *Vir Heroicus Sublimis*. This colossal orange painting deals with pictorial decorum in a new and radical way. The familiar agitated spatial movement and self-referring signs of Abstract Expressionist painting have been eliminated and grandly solemnized by a complex pulsation of high-keyed color over a pictorial field of vast expanse divided by two fine vertical bands. These fragile and oscillating stripes play tricks on the eye and the mind by their alternate compliance and aggression. Brilliantly visible and all but subliminally lost, they produce curious retinal afterimages. Their cunning equivocation quite subverts the idea of division and geometric partition, as if ideas of uniform space and mechanical analysis in a series were being swallowed by a new intuition of total experience. In this powerful and transfiguring visual drama, which has been aptly characterized the "abstract sublime," the enormous expanse of red becomes numbing to the ego, as any "oceanic" experience in nature moves us off our ego center; at the same time, the experience is mentally rousing since problems in visual interpretation are posed and require mental alertness. Newman's sources are momentary like Pollock's, despite his insistent geometry, and take account of psychological content.

The stern rigor of form, mechanical handling of surface, and problematic character of Newman's painting today can be seen to be related to the "anti-sensibility" painting of a whole school of younger abstract painters, and even to the bright, unmodulated surfaces of the Pop artists. Something of the same calculated insensitivity, directed to a higher artistic purpose, is also apparent in the paintings of Clyfford Still, whose preferred forms were organic, or biomorphic rather than geometric. His space-absorbing areas of homogeneous hue, whether bright or somber, his destruction of Cubist structuring and linearity, his rejection of facility in handling have had their considerable impact on the course of American art; in certain areas he was prescient and profoundly influential. Sam Francis's dripped, liquid paint applications owed something to the controlled accidents of Pollock's characteristic spatter technique, but when in his early style Francis massed his congested and dribbled kidney

shapes in curtains of luminous darkness, relieved only by the marginal activity of brilliant touches, his main artistic debt was to Still. As early as the mid-forties, Still had experimented with radical chromatic reductions, pushing color expression close to invisibility by loading his canvas with opaque blacks and purples, and keeping in play only a thin and aberrant fluctuation of bright spectrum color at the extreme edges of the canvas rectangle.

The reductions of chromatic expression to near-invisibility have occurred in the fifties most dramatically in the black canvases of Ad Reinhardt. His segmented, compositional grids are so dark and even in emphasis that distinctions of form and color require the most intense scrutiny to be discovered. Yet the almost imperceptible movement the eye is allowed from one gestalt structure of geometric shapes to another and the shifts from color to its absence reconstitute, in quintessential, expressive form, ideas of change and stability, activity and quiescence that are at the heart of the most significant contemporary expression. The single-mindedness of Reinhardt's means, the stately presence of his impassive icons and their painstakingly worked surfaces together comprise the most extreme example of purity in contemporary American painting. In their context of renunciation and austerity, faint tremors of personal sensibility, as they can be discerned under proper light conditions, register with added force and poignancy.

Division Among the Artists

The division among the Abstract Expressionists between an art of energy and impassivity, of impulse and sensation, was already apparent to many observers in the fifties, among them Professor Meyer Schapiro, who lectured on the new painters in 1956 in London. His remarks were published in a revealing article in the BBC *Listener.* There he contrasted Pollock and de Kooning's restless complexity to Rothko's inert and bare painting. "Each," he wrote, "seeks an absolute in which the receptive viewer can lose himself, the one in compulsive movement, the other in all-pervading, as if internalized sensation of a dominant color. The result in both is a painted world with a powerful immediate impact." The significance and influence of the less dramatic and obviously less "existential" painters, like Still, Rothko, and Newman, was limited by the extraordinary widespread impact of de Kooning on second-generation American artists. It wasn't really until the sixties, when the momentum of conventional action painting began to run down, and a younger generation of more objective tendency emerged, that the search began for different antecedents in the past. The paintings of Barnett Newman, Mark Rothko, Ad Reinhardt, and Clyfford Still certainly had their own appreciative audience and admirers during the fifties among the older avant-garde generation and on the West Coast around San Francisco. They acquired a far more significant audience among younger artists in the sixties—with the decisive shift of sensibility away from an expressionist, gestural art to a more orderly and objective abstraction. Only now are we able to see how prophetic, how far ahead of their own time, were such phenomena as Newman's very narrow, vertical canvases that now seem directly related to "minimalist" art—to the "deductive" structures of Frank Stella, in Michael Fried's phrase—how drastic and original were the black-on-black, nearly invisible and monotonal structures of Ad Reinhardt, beginning in 1954. Perhaps even more remarkable were Robert Rauschenberg's adjoining panels of white canvas shown in 1951, and Ellsworth Kelly's horizontal arrangement of a sequence of red, yellow, black, white, and blue panels created in 1953, but not shown in New York for a number of years.

The fact is that criticism and esthetic theory lagged behind actual developments in art, the usual state of affairs in such matters. As late as 1961, H. H. Arnason proposed the term *Abstract Imagists* for artists who were not Expressionists, in an exhibition at the Guggenheim Museum, recognizing the fact that action painting did not necessarily describe or fit the work of such artists as Newman and Rothko and many younger artists working with hard-edges, unitary images, symmetrical form, and broad, undetailed expanses of flat color. In the early sixties there was a sharpening focus of attention on new "color-field" abstraction, both in criticism and in exhibition activity. Clement Greenberg proposed the color-image paintings of Morris Louis and Kenneth Noland, in particular, as alternatives to an exhausted expressionist art. In 1963 the Jewish Museum, in an exhibition obviously influenced by the Greenberg esthetic, defined the growing anti-de Kooning reaction under the title of "Toward a New Abstraction." Among the artists shown were Kelly, Louis, Noland, Held, Parker, and Stella.

By the late fifties the alternatives to action painting were sharply visible and at hand, accessible to the artists themselves. In the older generation there were the chromatic abstract artists, Newman, Rothko, Clyfford Still, and, just emerging in a significant public manner, Ad Reinhardt. There was also a new line of development entirely of stained color painting, which stood in deliberate opposition to de Kooning's brushstroke technique and action painting generally. The staining technique seemed to evolve through Sam Francis, or perhaps Helen Frankenthaler, to Morris Louis and it then took a more rigorous geometric form in the work of Kenneth Noland. There was also apparent an increasing interest among a large group of artists in symmetry, sharp and clear definition, immaculate surface, and formal order, to counteract the freewheeling invention, spontaneity, amorphous forms, and messiness of the action painters. Soon the phrase *hard-edge* became current and popular to describe such artists particularly as Ellsworth Kelly. His decisive development had taken place, interestingly enough, in Paris rather than in New York, removed entirely from the American experience and orbit of action painting. Other artists like Leon Polk Smith, Alexander Liberman, and Al Held constituted a loose group, or constellation of new Precisionists. The anti-expressionist reaction was based on a new respect for order and clarity, on an almost classical sense of art's possibilities. These new tendencies, however, were not dependent on the traditions of geometric abstraction or constructivist examples, deriving from Mondrian and Malevich; the renewed formalist abstraction had acquired a native accent and elements of psychological ambiguity in its order, as well as a scale and energy associated with action painting. However, in place of the Abstract Expressionists' drama of creativity, their "gestures" on canvas, and physical, kinesthetic engagement with medium, there was now a new central issue at the heart of innovating painting. The younger artists had made conceptualism and objectivity decisive and controlling ideas. Paintings were no longer "composed," inflected, or meaningful in any traditional or directly interpretable sense. Where Newman minimized the painting process and detail in order to emphasize the metaphysical and sublime implications, if you will, of his art, Reinhardt with equally stern and reduced means reversed the procedure, and thus came closer to the new spirit of the younger generation, by making dark, passive, and very specific paintings, close to invisibility. However, Reinhardt's mood of complete detachment can incite an equally complete involvement by the viewer willing to sacrifice the ordinarily expected titillations of art.

6   Even within the austerities, simplifications, and even uniformities of current

abstract styles in painting and sculpture, Newman and Reinhardt exert their very different influences, Newman toward romantic expansiveness, and Reinhardt toward a more self-contained, conventionalized, and repetitive, or serial, art.

In the sixties, anti-expressionist, or "post-painterly," abstraction can be classified generally in terms of a limited but useful number of categories as follows: 1) *Color-field Painting* includes the lyrical abstractions of Helen Frankenthaler and Morris Louis, the more rigorous forms of Kenneth Noland, and the tangible atmospheric color haze of Jules Olitski. 2) *Hard-edge Painting* is a term taken from a late fifties exhibition title and applies broadly to the geometric, or at least clearly contoured, forms of the painters Ellsworth Kelly, Leon Polk Smith, Al Held, and Frank Stella, among others. The term is not entirely illuminating and must stand for the moment to describe a more precisely engineered and calculated painting of immaculate surface that emerged, historically, just before 1960. 3) *The Shaped Canvas* includes artists like Richard Smith, Charles Hinman, Paul Feeley, and also Stella. All these classifications—color-field, hard-edge, shaped canvas—are listed in the chronological order in which they were brought before the public, either through exhibitions or critical texts. 4) *Monochromatic Painting* acknowledges the great influence of Ad Reinhardt and as a mode has been decisive in the development of such younger artists as Robert Mangold. 5) *Optical Painting*. This is, of course, the type of art based on perceptual dynamics and optical scintillations explored by William Seitz's museum exhibition of 1965, whose "masters" are Vasarely, Soto, and the American Josef Albers, with such younger American artists as Richard Anuszkiewicz also practicing this style with distinction. Visual effects in the work of many color-field and hard-edge painters like Gene Davis and Ellsworth Kelly, and even Rothko, Newman, and Reinhardt in his work before 1954, can be considered "optical," for this art, too, utilizes close-toned color contrasts, afterimages, subliminal or violent effects of surface, and thus powerfully activates vision as one of its primary intentions. Many of the classifications overlap, of course. The color-image painters and the artists who use close-valued color oppositions of a subliminal refinement, whether bright or dark, are related in their different ways to each other. The scientific interest and bias of the hard-core optical artists, however, has had only limited influence on major figures in American art. 6) *Serial Art* is the last category of recent abstract painting. This is an art of repetitive imagery, lacking formal diversity, with repeated runs or sets of images or abstract configurations. The use of uniform and modular forms in anticlimactic patterns of organization is more apparent and more radical in contemporary sculpture, but the tendency has affected painting as well. The young artists pursuing this direction show different intellectual interests and habits of mind, too. They are attracted to Wittgenstein and modern logic, mathematics and information theory, and they react to the rationalist intellectual modes that serve a complex, technological society. Serial forms are one more organizing principle, like so-called Minimal art or Primary Structures, which seem appropriate and applicable to the understanding of the work of such artists as Larry Poons, Donald Judd, Sol Lewitt, Robert Smithson, Robert Morris, and some Pop artists, too, like Andy Warhol, who use repeating, mechanical imagery.

As early as 1954, Morris Louis's so-called floral paintings, which derived in turn from Helen Frankenthaler's first "soak-stain" painting—her abstract landscape of 1952, *Mountains and Sea*—announced an influential, new direction in art. Pollock or de Kooning's energetic drawing in paint and linearism were supplanted by large, more quiescent shapes and fields of thin color. The use

7

of paint as a dye rather than a paste by Louis and its application with the aid of gravity by tipping the canvas suppressed the visible effects of the hand of the artist; the hand was no longer felt, as in de Kooning, in terms of pressure or resistance of surface, and thus paint was seen as phenomenon rather than gesture — with a new clarity and objectivity. Louis's veils and overlapped washes of thin color led in due course to the structural rigor of Kenneth Noland's targets, chevrons, diagonals, and other emblem forms. There was, then, a progression from a lyrical art to new iconic form, away from accident, and profusion of means to symmetry, codification of gesture, and economy of means. Noland's work shows more intellectual rigor than Louis's art, which is more hedonistic and attuned to sensation. Noland's forms and signs are clearly defined, simple, almost banal in fact, but his color bands expand to the limits of his field and create an alternating current between focus and dispersion, between concentration within the emblem form and the sense of chromatic energies beyond their framing rectangle.

Kelly's hard-edge forms are scrupulously clean of detail and surface irregularity that would betray the individual hand or accident. The idea of chance or irregularity was once equated with personal authenticity. Formal decorum, however, came to seem both more honest and charged with expanding possibilities for the younger generation. Kelly managed a great variety of formal invention and a new kind of sensuousness within his stricter forms; figure and field each become a tangible reality, and the simplest facts of color and form are given immense, new, expressive powers.

In their shaped canvases, Stella, Richard Smith, and others created a nonrelational painting opposed to the expressionist art and two-dimensional pictorialism of the action painters. Their work emphasized the ambiguities between the pictorial and the structural, between visual illusion and three-dimensional object. The contoured stretcher provided one kind of definition, and painted forms, related to the stretcher but not bound to it, made another interacting image and visual metaphor. Stella's shaped canvases were created in various permutations and series, sometimes with alternate color schemes. The almost "idiot" simplicity of his composition or design stressed a purposeful blankness of mind, and hence gave further emphasis and meaning to the idea of the painting as an "object."

Beginning with Yves Klein in Europe and Ad Reinhardt in America in the middle fifties, color became an increasingly problematic aspect of painting. The audience's commitment to art was tested by bringing them as close to the contemplation of nothing, of an undifferentiated color rectangle, as possible. By insisting on boredom, and reducing their art content to a "minimal" point, these artists aggressively challenged their audience. As so often has happened in modern art, one impulse invited its contradiction, or its opposite, as a way of defining itself. Therefore the emphasis on vivid, brilliant color invited the cancellation of chromatic sensation altogether. Klein's effulgent blue monochromes and Reinhardt's blue and red single-color paintings led remorselessly to his "black painting," in effect, to anti-painting, as it seemed. The almost uniform, uninflected, and homogeneous quality of Reinhardt's black paintings, beginning in 1954, was very much related to the "single image" and the wholistic effect of much of the new contemporary abstraction that followed. In fact, it was this aspiration to a totality of vision, discarding detailed definition of parts, that most strongly characterized the reaction to the Abstract Expressionism of de Kooning, Pollock, Kline, and their orthodox followers among the action painters.

Op Art

Vasarely, Albers, and other optical artists, so-called, concerned themselves with perceptual dynamics and with the possibilities of color images that could be pushed toward subliminal brightness or, alternately, toward invisibility. Aggressive confrontation of color created pulsations of light and movement and intensified effects of fusion or dispersion, making of the canvas surface an extremely lively phenomenon and thus activating perception. At the same time "Op Art" of this type also has a problem-solving character that involves the audience in new modes of interaction with the work of art in puzzling out its governing system. It is a modified form of game-playing and puzzle-solving. However, the extremely scientific and even mechanical aspect of Optical Art, its almost exclusive emphasis on retinal reactions and sensation, limited its expressive range. As a style of expression, it found more sympathy in Europe than in America, perhaps because it was based on precedents in constructivist and kinetic art that had more deeply rooted European traditions.

Serial art and new minimalist and structurist forms combine the illusionism, which Optical Art made a game, with severely reductive, formal, or structural elements. It was Stella who described his work as an impassive object and refused to submit it to interpretation, insisting only on its lack of associational or other expressive content. He and many of the artists who have been described as minimalists in painting and in sculpture—Darby Bannard, Larry Zox, Ronald Bladen, Robert Morris, Donald Judd, Dan Flavin, and others—share the common characteristic of using extremely simplified forms, either in the single concentrated image configuration or in serial runs or sets. Often the sense of the form and its contents do not coincide; in fact, a bland and neutral-looking, geometricized object may be the vehicle for an aggressive assault on the spectator, through dazzling color combinations or cunning twists of form in space or architectural scale. The repetition of imagery and the element of deliberate boredom are also aspects of contemporary film, dance, and music. These devices are both cathartic, as a way of purging the old sentimental content from art, and formally innovative in the new focus of vision they provide.

Art of a rudimentary character attacks the pretentions of "high" culture, and it also puts its audience on its mettle by testing the sense of commitment to art. This new collective sensibility presents us with the curious paradox of young artists who are making deliberately vacant or inexpressive art, and thus freeing themselves from nonessentials, in order to liberate a new kind of formal impulse. It is in the negative character of the serial repetitions, reductive or rejecting forms of the young that a relationship can be established to such a difficult artist of the older generation as Ad Reinhardt. As has been true so often in the past, a new esthetic came into being and expressed itself first simply as a reaction to the past; its positive assertions and discoveries were obscured in the beginning by its negations—the destructive impulse and iconoclasm we so often have encountered in modern art. With the minimalist and structurist artists today, one was almost more aware of the Dadaist elements of irony, mockery, and inflation in their forms than of factors of formal control, mastery of space and scale, new techologies in materials, powerful architectural scale, and monumentalism. The shaped canvases, repeating, serial themes, and minimalist compositions of Stella—whatever their psychology of creation and apparent impassivity—are among the most innovatory and influential paintings made in America since the generation of the action painters.

The new swing to objectivism in abstraction, typified by the shaped canvases of Stella and the commonplace, emblematic forms of Noland, has its parallel in the development of a new spirit of Factualism, first in the critically important art of Jasper Johns, and then in Pop Art. All of these artists, both abstract or representational, conceived of their art less as a mode of revelation or self-discovery as the action painters had done than as a set of specific facts, or a carefully controlled and self-contained system. The first artist to prepare the way for this new spirit of realism was de Kooning, with his celebrated *Woman* series. His imagery had been taken from the billboard and commercial illustrations before being subjected to the artist's powerful and expressive distortions in paint. The *Woman* series evolved from a collage method that utilized the lipsticked mouths of advertising photographs in color, and an imagery that included Marilyn Monroe and other mass-culture female idols.

At just about the same moment historically, Larry Rivers, a second-generation de Kooning follower, began the process of reappraising the pictorial cliché with his bizarre work in 1953, *Washington Crossing the Delaware;* this large "salon"-type painting had been inspired by American folklore and a popular academic painting of the nineteenth century by Luetze, which every schoolboy knows by heart. Taking a scorned and banal theme, Rivers transformed it by expressive handling in the current mode of action painting, but he managed to stereotype action painting techniques and ideas around a different focal center. Thus began a shift in the center of gravity of art. Thanks in part to Rivers, the "cliché," or visual commonplace, entered American art with a vengeance in the late fifties, and a vernacular visual language drawn from popular sources began to establish itself as an underground movement in sharp opposition to the subjective preoccupations and idealism of the period's dominating "high" art of action painting.

De Kooning's "impurity," his inspired raid on the urban environment for imagery and hints of subject matter, his collage technique of lifting transfers of newsprint from the tabloids, and the digressive quality of his vision with its reliance on external stimuli as well as painterly impulse had directly sanctioned Rivers' experiments. But Rivers himself pioneered and made an original contribution by introducing recognizable subject matter in far more explicit terms than had de Kooning, at a time when such adulterations of abstraction were considered close to treasonable in the avant-garde. Subject matter of the commonplace, particularly in the realism of his *Birdie* period, and his later representations of themes freely transposed from photographic images and trademarks of commercial products anticipated and then coincided with the development of similar content that had more far-reaching influence transmitted through the art of Robert Rauschenberg.

Rauschenberg worked in the early and middle fifties with the free brushstroke of de Kooning's action painting, but he began to load his paintings with rags and tatters of cloth, reproductions, comic-strip fragments, and other collage elements of waste and discarded materials of a Dadaist nature and density. His packed, agglutinated surfaces were worked over with paint in the characteristic gestural language of action painting, but painterly expressiveness had reduced prerogatives in the context of an artistic structure choked with alien matter. The intensified use of subesthetic materials called into question the hierarchy of distinctions between the fine arts and extra-artistic materials drawn from the urban refuse heap. "Junk Art" gathered momentum in the late fifties and in the sixties, and was given added emphasis in the conglomerates of rusting boiler and machine parts of Stankiewicz's sculpture, the surfaces of splintered wood and plastic of Robert Mallary, and in Chamberlain's crushed and shaped auto-body parts. Allen Kapprow, one of the prophets and advocates of literal experience in art, proposed "a quite clear-headed decision to abandon craftsmanship and permanence," and "the use of obviously perishable media such as newspaper, string, adhesive tape, growing grass, or real food," so that "no one can mistake the fact that the work will pass into dust or garbage quickly."

The junk materials that Rauschenberg and others incorporated into their work had a subversive content in glorifying what is destitute, outlawed, and disreputable. Such strategies not only posed questions about the nature of the art object and the integrity of medium but also commented on the social context of city life and mass culture that gave rise to such assimilations. Rauschenberg radically deepened the alliance with the image-world of popular culture and with artifacts of daily life, by inserting whole Coke bottles, stuffed animals, rubber tires, as well as miscellaneous, deteriorating debris into his work, and against these rough intrusions, painterly qualities characteristic of Abstract Expressionism operated. Unlike the poetic objects of the Surrealists, his debris was not calculated to shock by its incongruity; its associational or fantastic meanings, in fact, were underplayed and minimized. Junk and artifacts were used in an optimistic matter-of-fact spirit; if social commentary were part of their content, it was on an elementary and unspecific level, referring to nothing more than the life cycle of objects in our culture, and their rapid decline into waste as the flow of new goods pushes them aside.

The innovations of Jasper Johns have had an even more far-reaching influence on the radical changes that took place in the sixties. His historic paintings of flags and targets, first exhibited in 1957, and the subsequent maps, number series, rule and circle devices, and other themes created radical new forms of representation, utilizing commonplace imagery. Many of his subjects elucidated the creative process in a "do-it-yourself" spirit, breaking down and isolating constituent parts of illusion and literal fact, the visual and the tactile, and inviting the public to restructure the magical unities of the esthetic experience. Johns's American flags, in particular, showed new and startling possibilities of image-elaboration by making over the devalued currency of a visual cliché that seemed empty of content due to over-familiarity. As Abstract Expressionism and its cult of the work of art as a unique, privileged experience became stereotyped in the hands of academic followers, the commonplace image took on fresh possibilities of expressive life. The most inventive artists began to manipulate the least "interesting" subject matter and make of it the most interesting new forms in the sixties.

Johns's first characteristic and innovatory image was the target. In two separate versions, fragmentary, painted casts of body parts and a repeated partial mask of the face were set in a series of open boxes over a centered bull's-eye. The sober formality of his hypnotic bull's-eye and the subdued human associations of his casts created a powerful interplay of thwarted alternatives. Human feeling and associations were suspended, in effect, between waxwork casts and a severe geometric and optical system. The body's cage and a mental prison were joined, and either image system proved curiously opaque and enigmatic. One expected to be able to decode messages from secret regions of the psyche, but they were effaced in "impersonality" in the received and sanctified modern fashion.

James Dine occupies a unique position among the artists emerging after 1960 who have been associated loosely, and in his own case erroneously perhaps, with Pop Art. His painting with object attachments and his environments have

11

an abrupt, muscular power that rebukes the indirection and muted poetic sentiment of his first mentor, Jasper Johns. Dine extends the paradoxical play between literal experience and illusionistic representation by regenerating, with a rivaling skill, the painterly direction of action painting, and then assimilating it to a wide repertory of objects rich in human association of personal use or admired strength. His household furniture, room environments, bathroom cabinets, tools, palettes, and robes are meant to be enjoyed for their expressive power within the formal scheme of his constructions. They are not underscored for their scandalous potential, but they do strike an overt, aggressive, not (an axe plunged in a log, a saw bisecting a blue field of paint) often released erotic fantasy. Dine's unvarnished directness and mechanical resourcefulness are in the American vein, more related in temper to David Smith than Johns, and thus free of the Hermetism that has been one of the liabilities of Johns's style for those who followed him too closely.

Claes Oldenburg is a sculptor, but he has had such a wide influence on all media and forms of art that he deserves special attention even in an essay devoted to painting. His extensive interests and energies make him one of the most important innovators of the sixties. He was educated, in effect, by Abstract Expressionism but broke with that movement around 1959, opening paths to a variety of new expressions, including Pop Art. He originated (with Allen Kapprow, Jim Dine, and Robert Whitman) the "happening," which extended action painting into a form of spontaneous, expressionist theater, but he is best known for the gigantic ersatz food in painted canvas and plaster that he evolved after 1960. The surfaces of these bloated facsimiles of the lunch and drugstore counter were at first freely handled in the splatter and splash technique of action painting, but the reference to their real-life models was clear and inescapable. A repeated emphasis on foodstuffs seemed rather innocently to draw on the preoccupation of advertising with the infantile oral obsessions of Americans, and Oldenburg's subject matter became the basis for similar themes handled in the more conventional terms of easel painting by Wayne Thiebaud and others. Oldenburg also created a series of free, painterly translations of commercial trademarks in dripping color and papier-mâché relief, among them *Seven-Up,* in vast enlargement. His themes were the consumer commonplaces of standard brands, but his handling remained deliberately chaotic and rather low in legibility like action painting, in this first period of his mature invention.

In recent years, Oldenburg's objects have been renovated, and they now "improve" on man-made nature. A series of soft telephones, toasters, typewriters, fans, and automobiles look freshly manufactured, slick and grossly opulent instead of overripe or decayed. The object is made slick and mechanical, something to be consumed by use rather than assimilated physiologically. It enters into the context of art as a newly minted, vinyl-covered object, before it has been caught up in the consumer cycle from use to junk. But these creations remain as outrageous as ever, both in their immensity of scale and their contradiction of the normal properties of the things they imitate and dissemble. We identify telephones by their hard and metallic shell, but Oldenburg's are collapsed and baggy, all epidermis and no working parts. They seem to stand on the threshold of animistic and magical life, but they never do slip out of their utilitarian identity, and this fine nuance is their whole point. For, like a deflated football, they are objects without a function. By taking them through such a poetic metamorphosis and making them useless, Oldenburg associates his telephones, typewriters, and appliances with the art object that is by definition *gratuitous*. His dummies, duplicates, and substitute objects create a rich play of shifting identities, which enters the very fabric of the art object itself and its fabricated, synthetic surface.

In the sixties, the increasing rate of technological change and the proliferation of mass communications converged with the diminishing momentum of the Abstract Expressionist movement to bring to birth an entirely fresh movement in American art. The communications industry, ever expanding, and occupying if not monopolizing public consciousness, directly precipitated those original forms of expression known as Pop Art.

Pop Art

The Pop artists take their imagery literally from the world of popular entertainment and from commercial sources. The imitative forms and familiar content of Pop Art have been the subject of acrimonious dispute among artists of the older generation, especially because, it has been charged, they do not expand sufficiently on their original, visual sources. Pop Art also seems to confirm all the mechanical and anti-individualistic tendencies in American life and culture to which the Abstract Expressionists, by contrast, proposed a loud and violent dissent. Since Pop Art is generally too "cool" to be subversive of the established order—a rule to which the explicit eroticism of Tom Wesselman's *Great American Nude* series is an exception—it has also been criticized as the Neo-Dada of the "age of affluence." The older avant-garde audience, feeling its values threatened, obviously preferred a restricted view of Pop Art as an entertainment.

Pop Art made its dramatic public debut in 1962 with the individual exhibitions of Roy Lichtenstein, James Rosenquist, Andy Warhol, Tom Wesselman, and Robert Indiana. An offending shock was experienced by many artists and almost all critics confronted by an imagery that scarcely seemed to transform its sources in the newspaper comic strip (Lichtenstein); the billboard (Rosenquist); repeating or isolated commercial brand symbols (Warhol); montage in strong relief of food products (Wesselman). The more obviously esthetic intention of Robert Indiana's lettered signs and directional symbols was found only slightly more acceptable, since he, too, took over explicit and routine commercial or industrial imagery, road signs, and mechanical typefaces. Image banality was matched, as a source of provocation, by the apparent indifference of Pop artists to individualized handling, and their uncritical enthusiasm for the bald, visual stereotypes of commercial illustration. Mechanical image registration in current styles of commercial art ran strongly counter to the accumulated store of knowledge, craft, and painterly expressiveness built up by a previous generation. High art culture was prepared for expressionistic rawness in art, but slickness seemed intolerable and was considered meretricious.

With the passage of time, however, it has become clear that the Pop artists were genuine and powerful innovators, and their work can even be related in style to current modes of hard-edge and optical abstraction. Most significantly, their interest in the mass media can now be understood as selective and discriminating rather than servile imitation, or mere documentation. Communications media are regarded as dynamic process and an environment rich in artistic metaphors and meanings rather than a source of style, content, and stereotyped techniques that were to be accepted uncritically and reproduced by rote. By monumentally dilating a detail, Rosenquist discovered iconic possibilities in a commercial sign fragment and created confusing, alternative readings of his compartmented paintings. They thus relate both to the ambiguous legi-   13 bility of contemporary abstraction and to the deliberate confusion of Surrealism. Lichtenstein slows down the cartoon image by enlargement, in effect; by overstating the Benday screen dots conspicuously as part of his form, he compels our attention to media and process as his primary content. His art is "about" art and style despite its mechanical look. Another kind of distance was achieved by Lichtenstein in his choice of somewhat out-of-date comics for his subjects. Modern life speeds up the sense of time's passage and makes us more sharply aware of changing styles, events, and the obsessional interest of public life with change and novelty. These intuitions are at the heart of much Pop Art. The communications media have become a collective vehicle of instant history making, contracting time and space into a blurry, continuous present, which makes even the recent past seem like events of ancient archaeology.

Warhol's repeating images of car crashes, movie stars, or soup cans are snatched from the march of news events, the daily unfolding of the celebrity pageant, or the life cycle of processed articles and food. The iconic gravity of his forms counters the accelerated transience of the journalistic ephemera that are fixed and symbolized. He has also constructed food and soap cartons of painted wood, stacked to imitate a supermarket storeroom. These objects exist by the slightest nuance of contradiction between the actual object and its simulations and the artist's fine calculation of his audience's different responses to each. Warhol destroys the functional and visual credibility of a store package whose legend, image, and shape we know by heart, but which we refuse to accept in the context of art. The original reality and its wooden painted dummy both float in our minds for an instant, in a kind of free-fall state without normal attachment. This is but another ingenious and effective way of elucidating in public the rudimentary alienations of artistic process and of inviting audience participation in that process. As the Impressionists mixed colors on the retina of the beholder's eye for greater immediacy, so Warhol mixes a known detergent or food package and its artificial facsimile in the mind, liberating a prepared image from the context of life into the context of art.

Robert Indiana's lettering and signs are organized in more traditional pictorial terms, but play on dual sets of responses both to verbal and visual information. His vivid optical flicker, dissonances, and emblematic forms scintillate and scramble and then unscramble color structures in a manner of abstraction that can be linked to an honorable paternity in Barnett Newman, Albers, and Vasarely. Indiana's precise shapes and optical color can be even more directly associated to the work of his contemporary, Ellsworth Kelly. Lichtenstein's parodies on Picasso's style, as well as the comic strip, and his abstract sunsets and "brushstrokes" energetically combine an intense estheticism with the mechanical kind of sensibility derived from "low" art that he has now firmly established as viable for "high" art. The monumentality, formal power, and essential simplicity of Pop Art links it directly to the most ambitious forms of contemporary abstraction rather than to an anecdotal realism of a more traditional and modest, formal character.

Of great interest is the character of the Pop artist's media sources. The TV screen, the advertising blowup, the blurred Wirephoto, the comic strip—all provide images relatively crude and low in definition, whose character as media is therefore more emphatic and visible. Marshall McLuhan, a brilliant analyst of the revolutionary impact on human perceptions of mass communications media, has noted that such "low-grade" imagery, low in content and information, "share a participational and do-it-yourself character." The imagery and conventions that Pop Art draws on are both "cool" and dynamic, coarse and unfinished, despite their mechanically processed look. They require audience activity and fill-in, and constantly recall their own character as an expressive process. Somewhere in the background of Pop Art is lodged a critical awareness of the tendency of mass media toward repeatability and uniformity, and a sense that the vast flow of duplicates and fictions in the "media" compromises the very idea of the "original." The reproduction process, then, is very much part of the assigned intellectual content of Pop Art.

Today, the sociologist Daniel Boorstin points out that the "original" has acquired a technical or esoteric status as mere prototype or matrix from which copies can be reproduced. A public that cheerfully accepts Van Gogh's *Sunflowers* in countless reproductions may be quite unprepared for the demands on individual response required by its obscure and scarcely known original. The printing revolution and the more recent flood of pictorial reproductions helped dispel the notion that uniqueness was indispensable to art, and thus created, along with other elements of urban mass culture, a new alternative "low" popular tradition to high art. The Pop artists, however, do not merely repeat the forms and content of mass media but select certain significant aspects and then transform them. The color surfaces of Rothko, Still, and Newman, and their perceptual ambiguities, the "environmental" emphasis of so much current art, beginning with de Kooning and given greater emphasis by Rauschenberg, Johns, and Oldenburg, and their standardization of individual handling—all these factors have prepared the way for the vital, new assimilations of the stereotyped forms of popular and commercial art. Another fascinating and entirely native precedent has existed in American art for some time, anticipating the incorporation of visual clichés and lettering in an emblematic subject matter of standardization: the lively, brash vernacular style of Stuart Davis, who fused Léger's Cubism and the surfaces of American life so vividly in his own art.

No longer a faithful mirror of the world of popular culture, Pop Art lost momentum as a group style after 1965. Individual artists associated with it, on the other hand, have become increasingly resourceful, even if they seem to be losing touch with the original impulse that inspired them. Oldenburg, Lichtenstein, Indiana, Warhol, Wesselman, and Dine have all continued to develop and to expand their creative worlds in surprising ways. Oldenburg's "soft" forms are now a powerful influence on contemporary abstract sculpture; the ersatz, commercial surfaces and synthetic textures of Pop Art have directly affected other Abstract Expressionists, especially in sculpture, and encouraged new intermedia experiment. Reversing the process of influence, geometric and "minimalist" sculptural forms currently popular have also influenced a number of the Pop artists. There is in fact a very lively interaction between apparently antithetical modes of abstraction and the representationalism of Pop Art, to their mutual benefit. If this is true, and the results are as expansive and significant as one believes, then obviously the durability of the Pop artists, if not their original group style, is based on sound, formal values. Pop Art in America was always much more than shallow representationalism or comic journalism, as its detractors charged. The Pop artists include at least two major innovators in America today: Oldenburg and Lichtenstein. As has so often been true in the past, the work of these individuals has far transcended the apparent, circumscribed, expressive limits of the general movement that originally generated their work. The assumptions of Pop Art are no longer adequate to describe the work of these two artists, or their inventiveness and formal mastery.

Sculpture Replacing Painting

American painting today seems to be undergoing a more severe crisis than any since the war. The color-field painters, shaped-canvas makers, minimalists, and Pop artists are all suffering from the same malady — the exhaustion of those specialized conventions that define the modes of painting. The radical distinctions of even the recent past between painting and sculpture no longer hold true; each is rapidly becoming a hybridized version of the other, and sculpture, in its more severe, geometric reductions especially, has shown itself to be the most potent influence by far in establishing formal precedents and new conventions. Painting has drawn ever closer to sculpture, and in so doing, abandoned many of its old powers and prerogatives. It has given a more literal accounting of the painted surface as an object, without yet becoming an outright, freestanding, or necessarily sculptural form. On the other hand, artists who began as dedicated painters have now embarked on radical media experiments, in materials ranging from plastics to projected light. It all seems to comprise a deliberate campaign to dematerialize and desanctify the painting-object. Between such radical and devastating wrenches in opposite directions, painting has understandably shown neither a strong persistence in a single mode, with the possible exception of a small cluster of color-field painters, nor any very great stability.

There are a few signs, such as the last one-man shows of Larry Poons and the continuing viability of such lyrical abstraction as Helen Frankenthaler's, that a slight, but not decisive, resurgence in favor of "painterly" painting is in progress. However, the general tendency today is to seek radical redefinitions of different media, to test their content, values, and expressive means. In the face of these confrontations, painting as such has sought a new accommodation with, on the one hand, three-dimensional structure, and, on the other, intermedia experiment and new materials; both of these modes effectively destroy painting's traditional characteristics of concreteness and illusionism. Despite the inventiveness and importance of Johns, Noland, Kelly, Stella, Lichtenstein, and a few others, for the moment one is forced to conclude, on the evidence, that the most vital avant-garde expressions among the younger generation are in sculpture. Tony Smith, Judd, Morris, Oldenburg — and possibly Duchamp — have replaced Johns, Noland, Stella, and Kelly as the source of new impulses and vital generative ideas in American art. Art still flourishes in America — that is, art in the form of sculpture, conceptual art, and related projects — but painting as such, at this moment, is facing nothing less than a mortal crisis.

PLATES

Action Painting and Abstract Expressionism

PLATE 1   ARŚHILE GORKY *Apple Trees*, 1943–46 (117 x 132 cm) Private Collection

PLATE 2   HANS HOFMANN *The Birth of Taurus*, 1945, Guilford, Connecticut, Collection of Fred Olsen

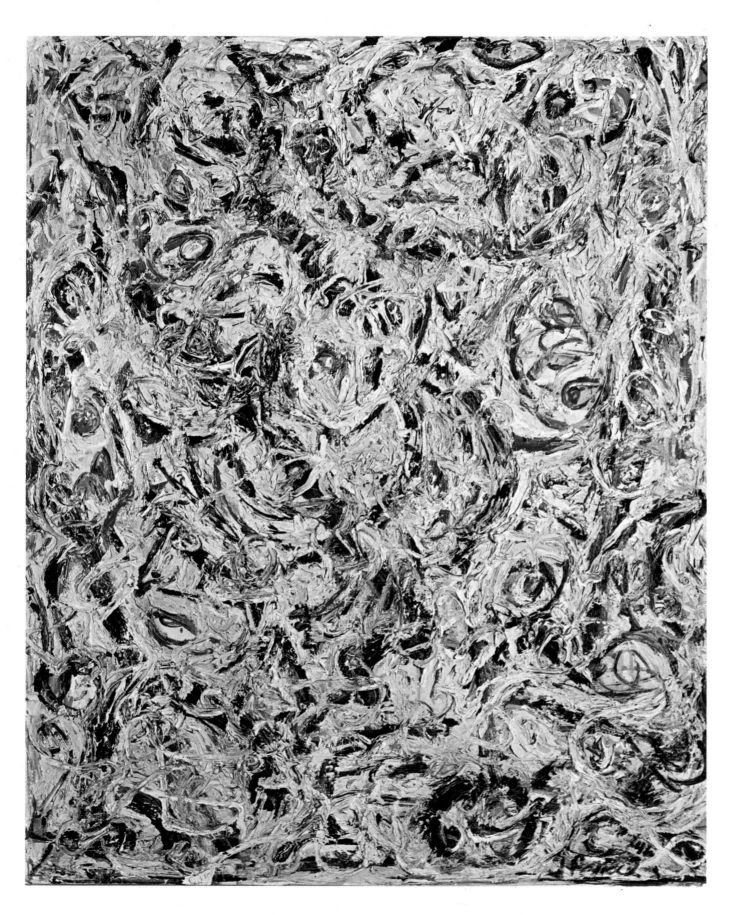

PLATE 3   JACKSON POLLOCK *Eyes in the Heat,* 1946 (137 x 110 cm) Venice, Peggy Guggenheim Foundation

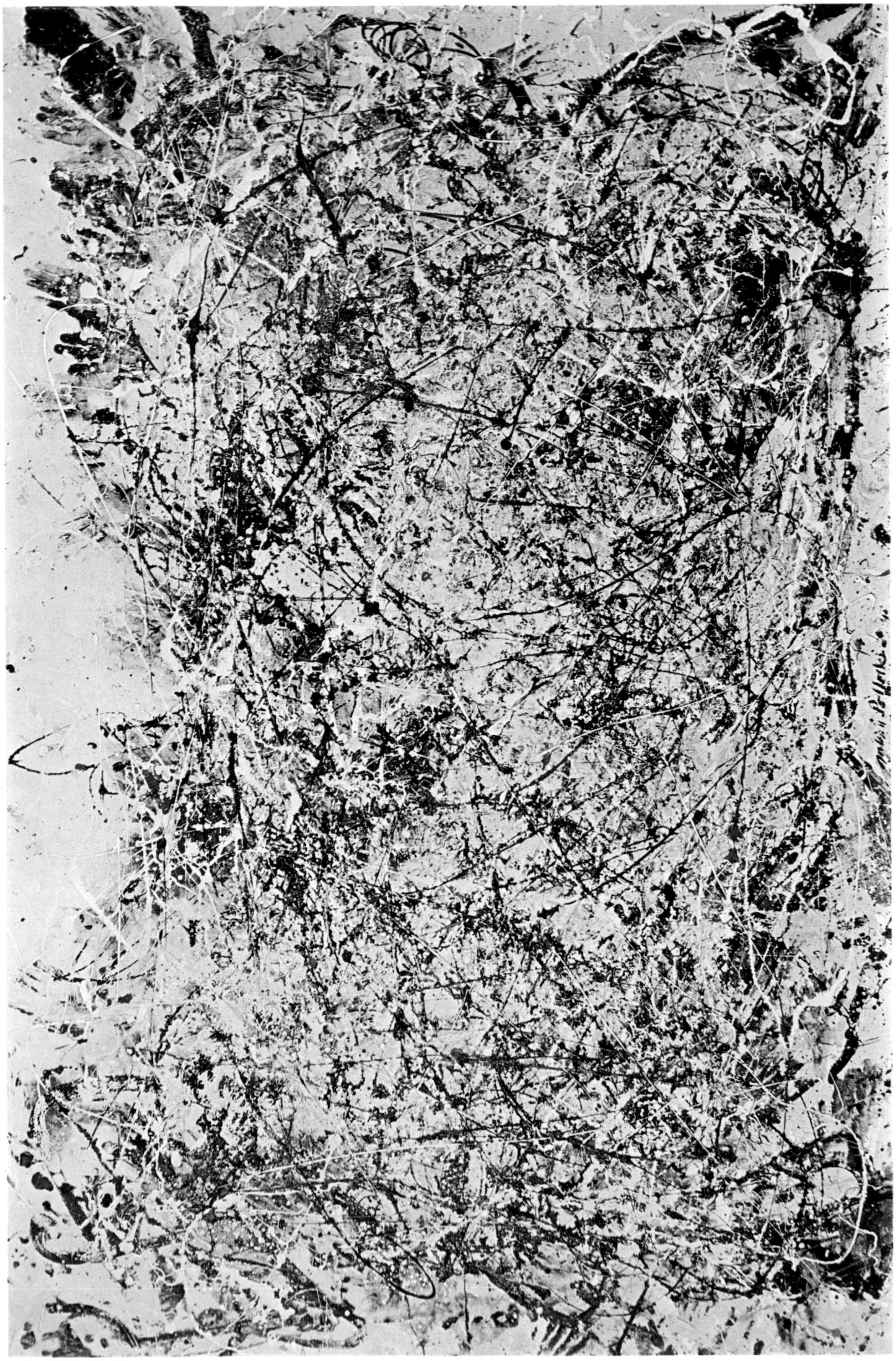

PLATE 4   JACKSON POLLOCK *Number 1*, 1948 (173 x 264 cm) New York, Museum of Modern Art

PLATE 5   JACKSON POLLOCK *Blue Poles*, 1953 (270 x 534 cm) New York, Collection of Mr. and Mrs. Ben Heller

PLATE 6   WILLEM DE KOONING *Pink Angels,* c. 1945 (130 x 100 cm) Beverly Hills, Collection of Mr. and Mrs.
Frederick R. Weisman

PLATE 7   WILLEM DE KOONING *Woman*, 1949 (153 x 121 cm) Hanover, Pennsylvania, Collection of Mr. and Mrs.
Boris Leavitt

PLATE 8   WILLIAM BAZIOTES *Cyclops,* 1947 (122 x 102 cm) Chicago, Art Institute of Chicago

26

PLATE 9   ROBERT MOTHERWELL *The Emperor of China*, 1947, Provincetown, Massachusetts, Chrysler Art Museum

27

PLATE 10   WILLEM DE KOONING *Excavation*, 1950 (203.5 x 254.5 cm) Chicago, Art Institute of Chicago

PLATE 11   WILLEM DE KOONING *Two Women in the Country*, 1954 (115 x 102.2 cm) Greenwich, Connecticut, Collection of Joseph
H. Hirshhorn

PLATE 12   WILLEM DE KOONING *Black and White, Rome D*, 1959 (98 x 70 cm) New York, Collection of Marie Christophe Thurman

PLATE 13   FRANZ KLINE *Monitor*, 1956 (200 x 294 cm) Milan, Private Collection

PLATE 14   STUART DAVIS *Something on the 8 Ball,* 1953–54 (56 x 45 cm) Philadelphia, Philadelphia Museum of Art

32

PLATE 15   MARK TOBEY *Above the Earth,* 1953 (100.3 x 76.5 cm) Chicago, Art Institute of Chicago

Abstract Symbolism

PLATE 16   CLYFFORD STILL *Painting*, 1949 (200 x 170 cm) Baltimore, Collection of Dr. and Mrs. Israel Rosen

PLATE 17   MARK ROTHKO *No. 26, 1947* (86.5 x 115 cm) New York, Collection of Mrs. Betty Parsons

PLATE 18   MARK ROTHKO *Golden Composition*, 1949 (168 x 105 cm) Private Collection

36

PLATE 19   AD REINHARDT *Yellow Abstraction*, 1947 (100 x 80 cm) New York, Collection of Mrs. Ad Reinhardt

PLATE 20   BARNETT NEWMAN *Euclidian Abyss,* 1946–47 (70 x 55 cm) Meriden, Connecticut, Collection of Mr. and Mrs. Burton Tremaine

PLATE 21   BARNETT NEWMAN *Dionysius,* 1949 (173 x 120 cm) New York, Collection of Annalee Newman

PLATE 22   BARNETT NEWMAN *Vir Heroicus Sublimis,* 1950–51 (212 x 285 cm) New York, Collection of Mr. and Mrs. Ben Heller

PLATE 23   MARK ROTHKO *Violet and Yellow on Rose*, 1954 (212 x 172 cm) Milan, Private Collection

PLATE 24   ADOLPH GOTTLIEB *W*, 1954 (183 x 91.5 cm) New York, Solomon R.
Guggenheim Museum

PLATE 25   ADOLPH GOTTLIEB *Pink Earth*, 1959 (152 x 92 cm) Brescia, Italy, Cavellini Collection

PLATE 26 AD REINHARDT *Abstract Painting*, 1956 (200 x 107.5 cm) New Haven,
Yale University Art Gallery

PLATE 27 CLYFFORD STILL *Picture*, 1957 (289 x 408 cm) Basel, Kunstmuseum

Toward a New Abstractionism

PLATE 28   SAM FRANCIS *Shining Black,* 1958 (201 x 134 cm) New York, Solomon
R. Guggenheim Museum

PLATE 29   PHILIP GUSTON *Duo*, 1961 (183 x 173 cm) New York, Solomon R. Guggenheim Museum

PLATE 30   JOAN MITCHELL *Looking for a Needle,* 1959 (116 x 89 cm) Milan, Private Collection

PLATE 31   LARRY RIVERS *It's Raining, Anita Huffington,* 1957 (260 x 213.5 cm) Washington, D. C., Smithsonian Institution, National Collection of Fine Arts

PLATE 32   HELEN FRANKENTHALER *Mountains and Sea,* 1952

PLATE 33   HELEN FRANKENTHALER *The Bay*, 1963 (205 x 207 cm) Detroit, Institute of Arts

PLATE 34   MORRIS LOUIS *Columns*, 1960–61, Washington, D. C., Collection of Mrs. Morris Louis

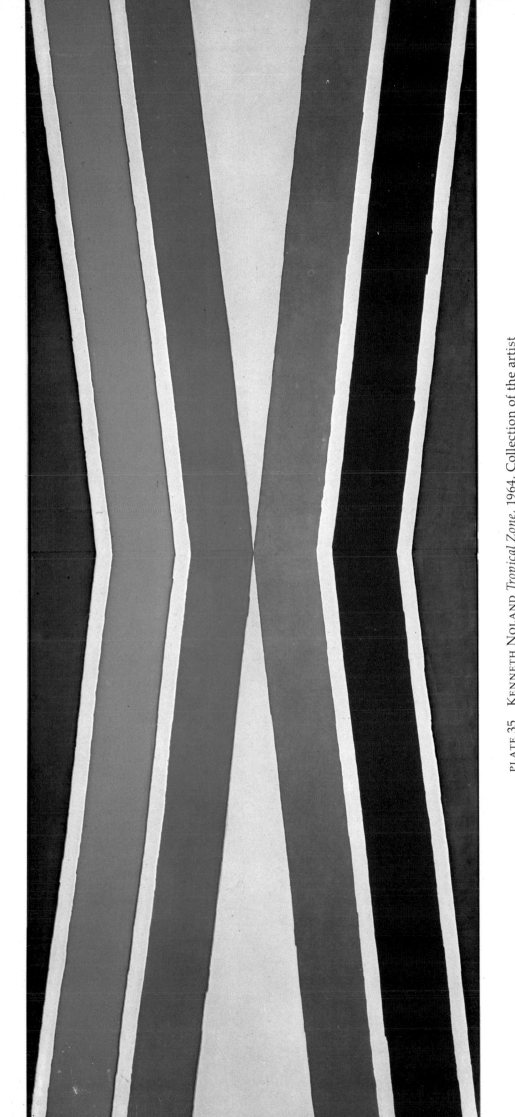

PLATE 35 KENNETH NOLAND *Tropical Zone*, 1964, Collection of the artist

PLATE 36   JULES OLITSKI *Surface Cause*, 1968 (117 x 282 cm) New York, Collection of Alexis Gregory

PLATE 37   ELLSWORTH KELLY *Blue Green*, 1968 (228 x 228 cm) Collection of the artist

PLATE 38 FRANK STELLA *Marrakech*, 1965 (192.5 x 192.5 cm) New York, Collection of Mr. and Mrs. Robert C. Scull

PLATE 39   FRANK STELLA *Hatra II*, 1968 (300.5 x 600 cm) Saint Louis, Collection of Joe Hellman

PLATE 40   JOSEF ALBERS *Homage to the Square,* 1962 (61 x 61 cm) New Haven, Collection of Carrol Janis

PLATE 41   RICHARD ANUSZKIEWICZ *Cadmium Yellow,* 1967 (60 x 60 cm) New York, Sidney Janis Gallery

PLATE 42   LARRY ZOX *Scissors Jack Series*, 1965–66, New York, Kornblee Gallery

PLATE 43   LARRY POONS *Painting*, 1968 (275 x 217.5 cm) New York, Leo Castelli Gallery

PLATE 44 RAYMOND PARKER *Pink*, 1968 (235 x 270 cm) New York, Collection of the artist

Op Art and Pop Art

PLATE 45   ROBERT RAUSCHENBERG *Curfew,* 1958 (145 x 99 cm) New York, Collection of
Mr. and Mrs. Ben Heller

64

PLATE 47   ROBERT RAUSCHENBERG *Third Time Painting,* 1961 (214 x 152.5 cm) New York, Collection of the
family of Harry N. Abrams

PLATE 46   ROBERT RAUSCHENBERG *The Bed,* 1955 (185 x 77.5 cm) New York, Collection of Mr. and Mrs. Leo
Castelli

PLATE 48 JASPER JOHNS *By the Sea,* 1961 (183 x 137 cm) New York, Collection of Mr. and Mrs. Robert C. Scull

PLATE 49   JASPER JOHNS *Diver*, 1962 (228 x 432 cm) Byram, Connecticut, Collection of Mrs. Vera G. List

PLATE 50 JASPER JOHNS *Field Painting*, 1963–64 (93.5 x 183 cm) Collection of
the artist

PLATE 51   JIM DINE *Shoe*, 1961, Collection of the artist

PLATE 52   ROY LICHTENSTEIN *Girl Drowning*, 1963, Seattle, Collection of Mr. and Mrs. C. B. Wright

PLATE 53 ROY LICHTENSTEIN *Untitled Landscape,* 1964 (40.5 x 61 cm) Brescia, Italy, Cavellini Collection

PLATE 54 ROY LICHTENSTEIN *Big Painting 6* 1965, New York, Collection of Mr. and Mrs. Robert C. Scull

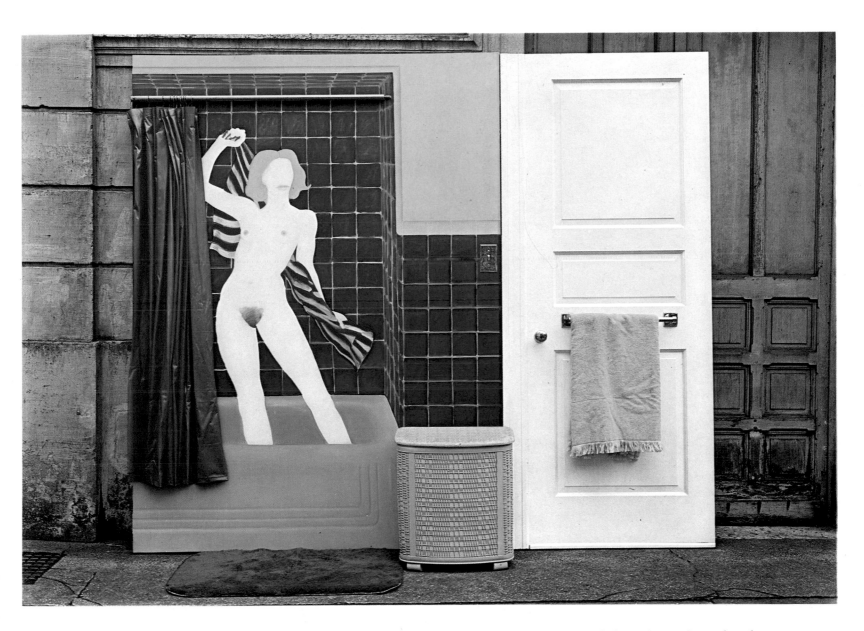

PLATE 55   TOM WESSELMAN *Bath Tub Collage No. 3*, 1963 (210 x 265 x 45 cm) Paris, Galerie Ileana Sonnabend

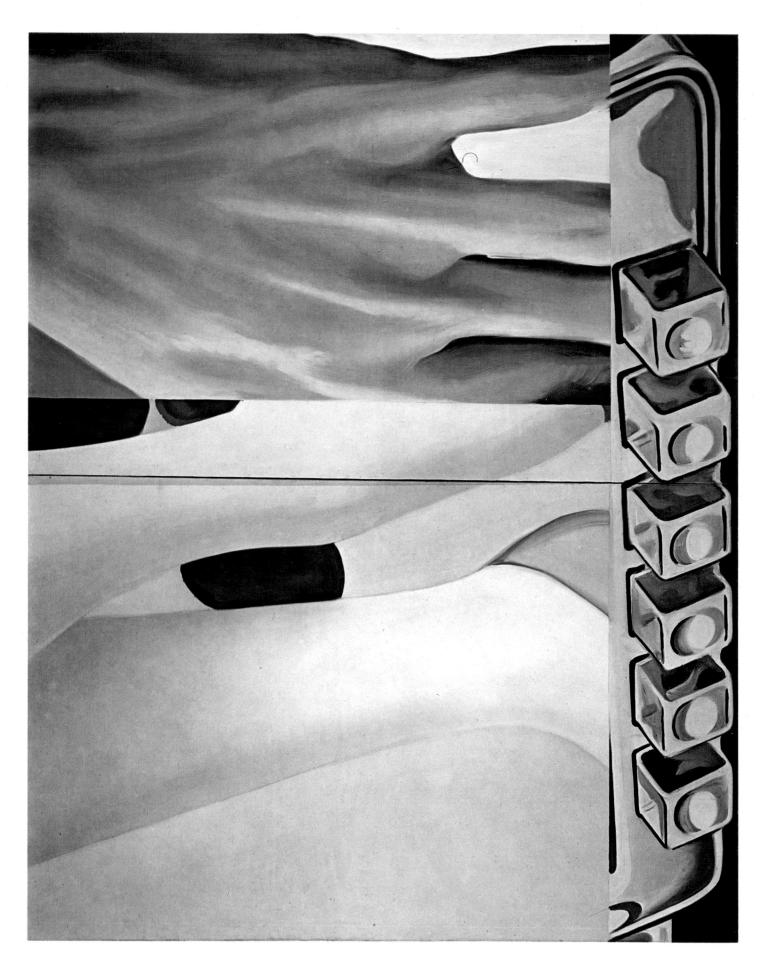

PLATE 56 JAMES ROSENQUIST *Push-Buttons,* 1960–61, Milan, Private Collection

PLATE 57   JAMES ROSENQUIST *Capillary Action 1,* Milan, Private Collection

PLATE 58   ANDY WARHOL *Green Coca-Cola Bottles,* 1962 (208.5 x 267 cm) New York, Whitney Museum of American Art

PLATE 59   ROBERT INDIANA *Untitled Serigraph*, Private Collection

PLATE 60   ANDY WARHOL *Big Flowers*, 1963 (122 x 122 cm) Turin, Galleria Sperone

THE ARTISTS

Photograph of Josef Albers

WILLIAM BAZIOTES

Born in June, 1912, in Pittsburgh. In 1933 he moved to New York and for three years attended the National Academy of Design. He devoted himself to teaching and his work, painting for the most part still lifes and landscapes. By 1939 his individual style was taking shape, and within two years his work was decidedly abstract. In 1948, with Motherwell, Newman, and Rothko, he founded the New York Subjects of the Artist School, which later became the Club, where artists of the avant-garde met every Friday. He taught at the Brooklyn Museum Art School and from 1949–52 at New York University. From 1952 on, he was on the faculty of Hunter College. He took part in many collective expositions in the United States and abroad and had one-man shows organized by Peggy Guggenheim, at the Galerie Maeght in Paris and at the Kootz Gallery in New York. He died in 1963.

JOSEF ALBERS

Born in Bottrop, Germany, in 1888. He studied art in Berlin, Essen, and Munich, and in 1923 entered the Bauhaus as a student, making his first explorations into the theme of the square. He taught at the Bauhaus until 1933, when the school was closed by the Nazis and he, and Bauhaus architects Walter Gropius and Ludwig Mies van der Rohe came to the United States. In this country he taught first at Black Mountain College in North Carolina until 1949, and from 1950–58 headed the Department of Design at Yale. Albers has been one of the most influential exponents of Bauhaus theories of functional design. His exhaustive studies of the visual effects of color, tone, and advancing and receding planes are perhaps best known in his famed *Homage to the Square* series of paintings and prints. He has exhibited throughout this country, in Australia, and abroad. He presently lives in Hamden, Connecticut.

MILTON CLARK AVERY

Born in Altmar, New York, in 1893, he grew up in Hartford, where he studied art for three years. He was, however, largely self-taught. In 1928, following his first one-man show in New York at the Opportunity Gallery, he exhibited regularly. A retrospective show was organized by the American Federation of Arts at the Whitney in 1960. He is known for his landscapes, which are often decorative with large or flat areas covered in bold colors. He lived in New York and traveled frequently, after his first trip abroad in the summer of 1952. He died in New York in 1965.

JAMES BROOKS

Born October 18, 1906, in Saint Louis. At ten he moved to Dallas, where he later attended Southern Methodist University. He came to New York in 1926 to study at the Art Students League. He painted frescoes for the Queensboro Public Library (1939) and for LaGuardia Airport (1942). He served three years in the Army. He later taught at Columbia University, and from 1948 to 1959 at Pratt Institute. In 1952 he received first prize at the Pittsburgh International Exhibition of Painting at Carnegie Institute, and in 1963 he was Artist in Residence at the American Academy in

BAZIOTES *Untitled*, 1946, Los Angeles, Collection of Mrs. Barbara R. Poe

Photograph of Willem de Kooning

Rome. From 1955 to 1960 he was at Yale University, in 1965 he was at the New College in Sarasota, and in 1968–69 he taught at Queens College. He lives in New York.

STUART DAVIS

Born in Philadelphia, December 7, 1894. One of the earliest abstractionists, he grew up in the company of artists. His father, Edward Wyatt Davis, as art editor of the *Philadelphia Press,* was commissioning illustrations from eminent artists like John Sloan, William Luks, Robert Henri, and William Glackens. At sixteen Stuart Davis entered the Henri Art School. He was an adventuresome seeker of new subject matter. For Davis the improvisational quality of jazz made it the only genuinely creative, modern form of expression in America. He exhibited five aquarelles at the Armory Show in 1913 and illustrated for *Harper's Weekly.* In 1917 he organized his first one-man show at the Sheraton Square Gallery. In 1931 he began teaching at the Art Students League. The following year he executed a mural for Radio City Music Hall. In 1940 he taught at the New School for Social Research and participated in several important shows. He took part in the retrospective exhibit at the Museum of Modern Art in 1945 and in the Venice Biennale in 1956. He died in 1964.

WILLEM DE KOONING

Born in Rotterdam in 1904. De Kooning came to the United States in 1926 and worked for a firm of commercial artists. He first supported himself as a house painter in Hoboken, New Jersey, before moving to New York. His friend John Graham, who was an influential theorist, was one of the first to recognize de Kooning's artistic gifts. He was supported as a full-time painter by the W.P.A. He worked for it in 1935, on a mural for the Williamsburg Housing Project (never executed), and assisted Fernand Léger on another unexecuted mural. Since that time his work has been on a relatively small scale. By the mid-thirties he was working on lyrical abstractions and a series of meticulous figure paintings and portrait drawings. By the mid-forties he was one of the major figures in New York artists' circles, and his stylistic and personal influences exercised considerable power over a younger generation of painters as well as his contemporaries. Although collectors largely ignored his work until the mid-fifties, he was included in many shows. His series of masterful black and white abstract canvases was exhibited

Photograph of Stuart Davis in his studio

DE KOONING *Fallen Angels,* 1965, New York, Allan Stone Gallery

in his first New York one-man show at the Charles Egan Gallery in 1948. By the fifties he had returned to the female figure theme (his *Woman I* painting)—a series of ambiguous, tortured-looking female figures and the theme of sexuality—and to broad, colorful, landscape-based abstractions. He has exhibited at the Janis Gallery, the Martha Jackson Gallery, and the Museum of Modern Art. He is the acknowledged *chef d'école* of one branch of the gestural tradition of Abstract Expressionism. He lives in The Springs, Long Island.

SAM FRANCIS

Born in San Mateo, California, in 1923. He attended the University of California, but his studies were cut short by the war. From 1943 to 1945 he flew with the United States Air Force, and did not receive his B.A. degree until 1949. In 1950 he moved to France to work and travel. He lived in Paris, traveling to India, Thailand, Hong Kong, Japan, and Mexico. In 1956 he was included in "Twelve Americans," a show held at the Museum of Modern Art in New York, and in 1958–59 he was one of eight painters chosen for the show "The New American Painting." His frescoes are in the Kunsthalle, Basel, Switzerland, and in the Sofu School of Flowers, Tokyo. He now lives in Paris.

ARSHILE GORKY

Born in 1904 in Khorkhom Vari Haiyotz, Armenia, the son of a wheat farmer and trader. The rich folk tradition of Armenia was to influence Gorky's later creativity considerably. He came to America in 1920 and lived in Boston and Providence, where he attended art classes. In 1925 he began to study at New York's Grand Central School, where he also taught until 1931. His works have been exhibited in the Museum of Modern Art, the Whitney Museum, the Mellon Galleries in Philadel-

phia, the San Francisco Museum of Art, and the Julien Levy Gallery in New York. In 1935 Gorky was employed by the W.P.A. to paint murals. In 1946 he appeared in the Museum of Modern Art's *14 Americans* show, but he was bitter about the terrible neglect he had suffered from museums, critics, and collectors throughout most of his career. In 1946 twenty-seven paintings were burned in his studio, and he underwent an operation for cancer; in 1947 he was injured in a car accident. He died in Sherman, Connecticut, in 1948.

ADOLPH GOTTLIEB

Born in New York, March 14, 1903. In 1920 he studied with John Sloan and Robert Henri at the Art Students League. In 1921 and 1922 he painted in Paris, Berlin, and Munich. Back in New York in 1925, he and Mark Rothko founded the group known as The Ten. In 1939 he accepted a commission from the Treasury Department, Committee of Fine Arts, to paint a fresco for the post office in Yerrington. He has taken part in group showings in the United States and abroad, among them "The New Decade," which the Whitney Museum sent to San Francisco, Los Angeles, and Saint Louis. He also organized his own one-man shows and collaborated on articles for *Art Journal*.

GORKY *Drawing*, 1947, Paris, Lam Collection

Photograph of Philip Guston in his studio

PHILIP GUSTON

Born June 27, 1913, in Montreal, he grew up in Los Angeles. Although he was largely self-taught, he did attend the Otis Art Institute in Los Angeles for a short time. In 1935, after about a year spent in Mexico, he moved to New York, where he worked for the Federal Art Project until 1940, painting murals for the New York World's Fair and for the Queensbridge Housing Project. In 1948 he won a painting fellowship from the John Simon Guggenheim Memorial Foundation, the Prix de Rome, a grant from the American Academy of Arts and Letters, and in 1958 a Ford Foundation grant. After this he traveled in Italy, Spain, and France. In 1941 he began to teach, first at State University of Iowa, then at Washington University in Saint Louis, and in 1950 at New York University. He has exhibited in the United States, South America, and Europe. He lives in Woodstock, New York.

HANS HOFMANN

Born in 1880 in Weissenburg, Bavaria, Germany. In 1896 he left home and enrolled in art school. In 1904 he studied at the École de la Grande Chaumière. He was friendly with the painter Delaunay and met Picasso, Braque, Matisse, and other Cubists. At this time he was painting still lifes, landscapes, and figure studies in a Cubist style. In 1910 he had his first one-man show at Paul Cassirer's Gallery in Berlin. In 1930 he taught for a summer at the University of California, Berkeley, and the next year at the Los Angeles Chouinard School of Art. In 1932 he closed the Munich School due to government hostility toward artists and in-

KELLY *Untitled*, New York, Collection of the artist

Photograph of Hans Hofmann in his studio, 1962

tellectuals, and he settled in America, teaching first at the Art Students League in New York. In 1933 he opened a school on Madison Avenue. By 1934 he had initiated the Hans Hofmann School of Fine Arts on Fifty-seventh Street, moving it downtown to Eighth Street in 1936, and also opening a Provincetown, Massachusetts, branch in 1935. By 1958 Hofmann had closed his schools to devote his time entirely to painting. His philosophy and teaching inspired a broad range of painters who studied at his schools, from the older, first-generation Abstract Expressionists to the younger artists who followed the example of de Kooning,

Pollock, and Still. Hofmann wrote about his esthetic theories in his book *Search for the Real and Other Essays*. He was one of the most influential of the European expatriate artists who came to America during the thirties and forties. He died in 1966.

ELLSWORTH KELLY

Born in Newburgh, New York, in 1923. He studied art at the Boston Museum of Fine Arts School. In 1948 he went to Paris, where he lived and worked until 1954, studying for a time at the École des Beaux-Arts. He returned to New York, holding his first American one-man show in 1956 at the Betty Parsons Gallery in New York. Kelly, the purest representative of hard-edge painting, has taken part in numerous exhibitions in the United States and abroad, among them the Venice Biennale in 1966 He lives in New York.

FRANZ KLINE

Born May 23, 1910, in Wilkes-Barre, Pennsylvania, he grew up in Philadelphia, where he later attended Girard College. In 1931 he entered the School of Fine and Applied Arts of Boston University, where he studied under Henry Heusche, Frank Durkee, and John Crosman, the last of these a noticeable influence on both the style and content of his painting. From 1937 to 1938 he was in London studying at Heatherly's Art School. He

Photograph of Franz Kline working in his studio

KLINE *Cardinal*, 1950, New York, Collection of Mr. and Mrs. George Poindexter

returned to New York, and from 1942 to 1945 he exhibited at the National Academy of Design. At this time Kline showed a growing interest in the work of several modern painters, Avery, Harthley, Tomlin, and de Kooning. In 1952 he began to devote himself to teaching, first at Black Mountain College in North Carolina and later at Pratt Institute and at the Philadelphia Museum School of Art. His work has been shown in many major exhibitions, and, in 1960, at the Venice Biennale. He died in 1962.

CONRAD MARCA-RELLI

Born in Boston in 1913, he spent part of his childhood abroad, returning to New York in 1926. He had his first private showing in 1948 at the Niveau Gallery in New York. When the Museum of Modern Art included his work in its traveling exhibition ''Recent Work by Young Americans'' in 1954–55, it described his painting as showing the influence of the Surrealists. He has been Visiting Critic at Yale University, University of California, Berkeley, and the New College in Sarasota, Florida. He lives in New York.

MOTHERWELL *Viva*, 1946, New York, Museum of Modern Art

ROBERT MOTHERWELL

Born in Aberdeen, Washington, in January, 1915. At fifteen he was able to draw anything, but his formal studies were not directed toward art. At Harvard University he studied philosophy, and in 1939 he attended Columbia University. He went to Europe in 1935; from 1937 to 1939 he attended the summer sessions at the University of Grenoble. On his return to New York in 1940 he decided to enroll in the Department of Fine Arts at Columbia, where he studied under Meyer Schapiro, who urged him to draw. He came in contact with a number of Surrealists, among them Tanguy, Masson, and Matta, the last of these being the most important to his development. With Matta, Motherwell traveled for about six months in Mexico, drawing and painting. He exhibited for

BARNETT NEWMAN

Born in New York in January, 1905. He studied at City College of New York and also at Cornell University. From 1922 to 1926, at the Art Students League, he studied with Duncan Smith, John Sloan, and William von Schlegel. He was a founder, with William Baziotes, Robert Motherwell, and Mark Rothko, of Subjects of the Artist School. He has shown his works in numerous exhibitions both in the United States and in Europe. He died in New York in July, 1970.

MOTHERWELL *Mural Fragment*, 1950, University of Minnesota Art Gallery (Gift of Miss Katherine Ordway)

NEWMAN *Genesis-The Break*, 1946, New York, Collection of Ruth Stephan Franklin

the first time in 1942 at the International Surreaiist Exposition in New York. His first one-man show took place in 1944 at the Art of this Century Gallery. Since then he has exhibited at shows and galleries throughout the world. He divided his time among painting, teaching, and writing. With Baziotes, Newman, and Rothko, he founded Subjects of the Artist School in New York in 1948. This later became the Club, where the avantgarde met weekly. He wrote for *Possibilities* and edited the series "Documents of Modern Art" (1944—52) and the first edition of *Modern Artists in America*. From 1951 to 1958 he taught at Hunter College in New York. He was at the University of Pennsylvania in 1962 and at Columbia University in 1964–65; since 1963 he has been an advisor to various reviews and institutions. At the present time he is general editor of "Documents of the Twentieth-Century Art" and advisory editor of *The American Scholar*. Motherwell makes his home in New York.

JACKSON POLLOCK

Born in Cody, Wyoming, in 1912. From 1915 to 1929 he lived in the West, in Arizona and California, studying painting and sculpture. He later studied with Thomas Hart Benton at the Art Students League in New York. For four years, 1938–1942, he worked for the Federal Art Project. In 1943 he had his first one-man show at Peggy Guggenheim's Art of this Century Gallery. His first abstract works date from 1945. Pollock was highly individualistic and particularly well known for his "drip" technique, with its superimposed layers of paint. His works have been exhibited in many galleries and museums in this

Photograph of Robert Motherwell

country and abroad. In 1945 he moved to East-hampton, Long Island, where he died in August, 1956.

ROBERT RAUSCHENBERG

Born in Port Arthur, Texas, in 1925. He completed studies at the Kansas City Art Institute and afterward attended the University of Texas. He spent several years in the Navy and then, in 1947, he went to Paris, where he attended the Académie Julien. He returned to the United States and studied at Black Mountain College in 1948–49 under Josef Albers, and then at the Art Students League (1949–50) with Robert Motherwell and Franz Kline. He traveled extensively in Italy and North Africa, returning to the United States in 1953 to settle in New York. He had had at that time three one-man shows, in New York, Florence, and Rome, and has since participated in numerous international exhibitions. He won first prize at the Venice Biennale in 1964. He was the designer and technical director for the Merce Cunningham Dance Troupe from 1955 to 1963. He now lives in New York.

AD REINHARDT

Born in Buffalo, New York, in December, 1913. He studied art history at Columbia University. In 1936–37 he worked with Carl Holty and Francis Criss at the National Academy of Design. He had his first showing in 1944 at the Artists Gallery. He spent the years 1944 and 1945 in the Navy, and upon his return once more took up the study of art history, this time at New York University. In 1947 he was made an assistant professor at Brooklyn College.

He taught at California School of Fine Arts, University of Wyoming, Yale School of Fine Arts, New York University, Syracuse University, and Hunter College. Reinhardt published several articles and exhibited in one-man shows and exhibitions in the United States and abroad. He died in 1967.

Photograph of Ad Reinhardt in his studio in front of his pictures

REINHARDT *Quadruptych*, 1959, Collection of Mrs. Ad Reinhardt

LARRY RIVERS

Born in New York in 1923. He served in the United States Air Force in 1942 and 1943, and on his return he studied at the Juilliard School of Music, playing professional saxophone with a jazz orchestra for two years on the side. He then began to paint, his formal studies first with Hans Hofmann in 1947 and 1948 and later with William Baziotes at New York University. He traveled in England, France, and Italy, and tried his hand at sculpture. He has had one-man shows and has taken part in many exhibitions. In 1953 he settled in Southhampton, Long Island, where he has continued to paint and sculpt, the latter work marked by figures with broad planes.

Photograph of Larry Rivers working on his composition

MARK ROTHKO

Born in Dvinska, Russia, in 1903. In 1913 his family left Russia to settle in Portland, Oregon. He entered Yale in 1921 and studied art. Four years later he moved to New York, where he painted for a short time at the Art Students League with Max Weber. He exhibited his work for the first time in 1929 at the Opportunity Gallery. His first private showing was held at the Contemporary Arts Gallery in 1933. Two years later he was one of the founders of the expressionistically inclined group The Ten. He has taken part in many important exhibitions and, in 1958, in the Venice Biennale. In that same year he began a series of murals commissioned for a large hall in New York. Rothko had also taught at Center Academy

of Brooklyn from 1929 to 1952, and in 1948 he was a co-founder of, and teacher at, the Subjects of the Artist School. He died in 1969.

CLYFFORD STILL

Born in 1904 in Grandin, North Dakota. When he was growing up, his family moved first to Alberta, Canada, and then to Spokane, Washington. He studied at Spokane University, where he received his B.A. degree in 1933. He subsequently taught fine arts at Washington State College in Pullman until 1941, when he moved to San Francisco and

Photograph of the studio of Mark Rothko, 1960
(Photo: Herbert Matter)

Photograph of Mark Rothko

practiced industrial design. He helped to inspire the Pacific (or West Coast) School. In 1944 he taught in Virginia, and in 1946 he returned to San Francisco to teach at the California School of Fine Arts (now San Francisco Art Institute) until 1950. He then moved to New York, where he taught at Hunter College and at Brooklyn College. Still has remained apart from the artists' group discussions and is quite independent in his art. He now lives in Westminster, Maryland.

MARK TOBEY

Born in Centerville, Wisconsin, in 1890. While still a young boy, he worked in Chicago and for a short time attended the Art Institute of Chicago, though he is for the most part self-taught. From

ROTHKO *Tentacles of the Memory*, 1945, San Francisco, Museum of Art

Photograph of
Bradley Walker
Tomlin

occasional trips to New York and Paris (1954–55). He was given a retrospective exhibition in San Francisco in 1951 at the hall of the California Legion of Honor and in New York at the Whitney Museum.

BRADLEY WALKER TOMLIN

Born in Syracuse, New York, in 1899, from a family of English and Huguenot origins. In 1921, having received his diploma from the College of Fine Arts at Syracuse University, he moved to New York. He won a scholarship in 1923, which enabled him to study in Europe at the Adadémie Colarossi and at the Grande Chaumière, and to work in France, Italy, and England until 1927, the year he returned to New York. From 1937 to 1941 he taught at Sarah Lawrence College in Bronxville, New York, and at roughly the same time he painted a mural for the Memorial Hospital in Syracuse. In 1924 he held a number of one-man shows: at the Montross Gallery, the Rehn Gallery, and, in 1950, the Betty

TOMLIN *The Armor Must Change*, 1946, New York, Collection of Mr. and Mrs. Ben Wolf

1911 to 1921 he lived in New York, where he received his first real encouragement as an artist with the exhibition of a series of drawings in 1917. He is considered to be one of the forerunners of Abstract Expressionism. In 1923 he taught at the Cornish School in Seattle. He moved to England in 1930 and traveled through Europe and the Orient. In 1934 in Shanghai he took a course from the Chinese artist Teng Kwei, mastering the rhythm and movement of the Chinese brush-stroke. Like Kline, he owes some of his rhythmic quality to Chinese calligraphy. He left England in 1935 and moved to Seattle to stay, except for

Parsons Gallery. His work is in the Addison Gallery of American Art, the Brooklyn Museum, the Phillips Gallery in Washington, and the Whitney Museum. He died in New York in 1953.

List of Illustrations

Courtesy Sonnabend Gallery, New York for the work of Jim Dine « Shoe »